A Message for Tomorrow's Leaders

Rosalyn Kahn

A Message for Tomorrow's Leaders

By Rosalyn Kahn

Published by Solutions Press

ISBN:978-0-9996497-9-4

This is a work of non-fiction. The ideas presented are those of the author alone. All references to possible results discussed in this book relate to specific past examples and are not necessarily representative of any future results specific individuals may achieve.

I love all the comments in this book, which are relevant to today's leaders.

Nick Delgado

Professor Rosalyn Kahn has assembled an impressive list of educators across all disciplines: body, soul, heart, mind, and spirit. They each make a compelling case to pursue lifelong learning as a fun, thrilling, rewarding discipline. If tomorrow's leaders embrace this poignant message, both they and our world will be happier, healthier, and much improved.

Dr. Ken R. Unger,
Founder and CEO of SoulDr.com

Dr. Unger is a Transformational Therapist, Speaker, Filmmaker and Best-Selling Author. He served on the White House Council on Families, won an Angel Award for Best 'Religious' show on Secular Radio, and was listed in Who's Who in America. In 2019 he received the Albert Nelson Marquis Lifetime Achievement Award.

What a great idea! *A Message for Tomorrow's Leaders* is right on time! The author's views allow students to have the desire to finish their education. I enjoyed reading each person's perspective! The key message is avoiding distractions, staying focused, finding your purpose, and being passionate about achieving your goals! Our goal is Peace, Freedom and Brotherly Love.

Joan E Wakeland, Retired Pharmacist, Distributor Bemer Group USA, ID # US 70761, Director, NAFE Riverside Connectors, Director, NAFE Hemet, Menifee Valley Lions Charter Member, Susan G Komen COP Advisory Council

This is an inclusive perspective on the importance of education and how humans thrive when we are more culturally intelligent. In addition, you have a diverse range of contributors that attest to your premise and highlight the need for education and leadership. Lastly, the text addresses the importance of communication and how this is essential to the growth of the individual and those around us. Overall, great work and I wish you the best!

Yeprem Davoodian
Department Chair,
Communication Studies,
Pierce College

A Message for Tomorrow's Leaders offers an eclectic view by various individuals who offer tools and hope during a time that needs healing. This collaboration, brought forth by Rosalyn Kahn, is a brilliant idea to bring diverse thinkers together and offer ideas that we can grow upon. Love, hope, altruism, freedom, and gratitude, all qualities we can find within happiness, are intertwined within the stories that are shared. Pain is our greatest teacher but it's appreciation of that discomfort which becomes the most powerful lessons that lead us to victory.

It is my fight in bringing people together as we can listen to the common saying that "we have power in numbers." I am an author, teacher, host of "Recovering Through Highness" which is to fight the stigma of substance abuse, but most importantly a student. This student mentality allows me to keep an open mind and continue learning. It is a book of inspiration that we all need so we can let down our guards and be ourselves.

Eric McCoy C.A.T.C II
Author, *Pain, Failure and Misery are the Stepping Stones to Success*
Host, *High While Clean* Podcast, Director of Education at New Creation College, Motivational Speaker, www.highwhileclean.org

When I read anything Rosalyn Kahn writes, I feel so much better because I understand what she tells us in her special, imaginative, spiritual, and magical way.

Many of us can take control of our own lives. By doing so, we have the chance to help others live their lives so much better, especially during this time of upheaval.

Rosalyn has a way of awakening our motivation to survive with less stress for whatever comes our way.

With the right choices, each of us can find the time to adjust our way of living to fit the circumstances in which we live during these pandemic months.

I find Rosalyn Kahn not only a most interesting person, but one who can see into our souls when she writes her books and communicates her findings.

Rosalyn's passion, dedication, and commitment to make the world a better place, one word at a time, makes her a unique and special lady.

Pink Lady Jackie Goldberg, Author
Get Up, Get Out, & Get A Life!

Rosalyn's book is a masterpiece of gaining a sense of the world in the pandemic from a diverse cross section of professions. Examining a historic moment, the advice is priceless for not only those in academia, but others as well to make sense and grasp our next step into today's changing times. It is a quick read but worth taking a closer look at the message. Rosalyn is on her third book and this one is certain to stand apart on its own. You will be glad you read it!

April Sellers
Nuri International

Having just read this compilation of encouraging accounts I can't help but think of the old axiom, "Facts tell but stories sell." We are all more apt to be moved to action from stories than facts and these are very inspiring stories indeed. Paging through the thoughts and experiences of these professionals will no doubt move our youth to embrace the benefits of an education. Kudos, Rosalyn, for the time, effort and passion it took to bring everyone together!

Ken Potter, RCP, RRT
Co-Founder, Bills To Blessings

Ros assembled a group of ordinary Americans to inspire tomorrow's leaders. For emergent changemakers, this quick read holds messages of wisdom and encouragement to reshape their world.

Kat Haber
TEDx Organizer

Rosalyn Kahn's compilation of words and wisdom from leaders across the globe captures snippets of advice and insight, with a focus on opportunities. The conversations with students come from a variety of people in all walks of life. A treasure for students indeed.

Mary Gallagher,
President Los Angeles City College

Table of Contents

Foreword
By John Bates

Leadership Communications Expert
CEO, Executive Speaking Success
TED/TEDx Speaker
Former TEDx Organizer and Coach to over 35 TEDx events

Whether you know it or not, no matter where you are in the hierarchy, you are a leader. At the most atomic level, you are always and at the very least leading yourself. And, because I know human beings and because you are reading this, I know you are a leader far beyond yourself as well. My question is: Are you aware of the power you wield as a leader and are you leading people in the direction in which you mean to be leading them? All around the world we see the impact of leadership, now more than ever. Great leadership and failed leadership are on display for all to see. The contrast is only more stark than usual. The clear lesson is: Never, never, never underestimate the power of leadership, the difference that leadership makes, and the difference you can make.

Rosalyn Kahn is a woman with a purpose and a message. For years I've watched her overcome obstacles, get back up when she falls, and never let anything stop her. It's inspiring and it is the secret to real success. Anyone who is successful will tell you success is just a series of failures in which you never gave up. Learn? YES! Pivot? YES! Stop? NEVER!

In October of 2000 my dot com company, after raising over $80M, failed. We went out of business and I almost died of an autoimmune disease brought on by the stress, the shame, and the sadness of that experience. I want to share with you the saying I heard later which I wish I had known then: *"There will come a time when you think everything is finished... That is the beginning."* - Louis L'Amour.

I thought that losing my company was the end. But, after falling, staying down, and crying for a while, I finally got back up. It turns out that was not the end, it was the beginning.

Rosalyn, too, has been through those moments of wanting to give up, to quit, to throw in the towel. She has always done the one thing it takes to succeed, get back up and keep going.

I hope you know that we are watching you. We know you are the leaders who will make the difference it will take to save human civilization and we are here to assist you. It's your future. It's your world and you're being handed a very wounded planet. I'm glad it's you, because I believe you are the ones who can turn things around and take all of humanity to the next level on a renewed planet.

Take the wisdom that speaks to you from this book and run with it. We need you and Rosalyn is standing for you, as are we all.

Foreword

By Christopher Salem

CEO of CRS Group Holdings, LLC
and Empowered Fathers in Action, Inc.

We live in a complex world where school environments today have become more diverse and high learning standards have set the vision of educational success for our youth. Our rapidly changing and more technologically oriented society will place higher demand for schools to create not only an ideal environment for learning but also an experience for our youth to apply this knowledge. The ability to apply knowledge to their skills and strengths will be necessary for them to do great things in our world and help them achieve success in life.

The role of leadership is more than just knowledge and theory to help youth help themselves to become tomorrow's leaders. It's the ability to empower our youth by leading through example. Schools going forward will be encouraged to find educators who can demonstrate the ability to connect, relate, and understand others in conjunction with their area of expertise with knowledge. Youths will be able to connect with educators at a deeper level based on similar values, effective communication that relates to them, and through transparent leadership. So why is this important? People in general, including our youth, want to feel others can relate and understand them where they are currently and are more likely to grow through an educator's example rather than just what was lectured to them. Moreover, educational leaders must recognize and assume a shared responsibility not only for students' intellectual and educational development, but also for their personal, social, emotional, and physical development. The increasing diversity of school communities places a premium on school leaders who can create a vision of success for all students, and use their skills in communication, collaboration, and community building to ensure that the vision becomes a reality.

Education plays an important role for change in a youth's life. It's the medium which can help them realize their true potential. Our education system must consider equipping our youth with the best possible education and establish favorable conditions to attain of their highest skills. This includes being an asset to the community and contributing actively to the development of the community.

In this globalized and knowledge-based world, our youth should be given the opportunity to contribute to the society while fulfilling their potential. Since education, as conceived of, seeks to change the way one lives and thinks, the youth first must be provided great educational opportunities and suitable conditions. The hurdles in their way to educational ends ought to be removed. Only then will the youth be a benefit to the community. The self-development of the youth is directly tied with that of each of us being responsible for our roles and duties that contribute interdependently to society. Being the example or leading by example helps others to change the paths of their own lives, where one must first start from him or herself. Beginning with self-awareness, our youth can strive to move forward, both flourishing and prospering. When our youth go to school, they can learn about their society, environment, social ethics, values and so on. It is incumbent on everyone in their communities to create constructive conditions for the youth to receive an education.

It is with the help of education that our youth can choose and act on their interests. They can choose their own way and direction in life. With this, they can set goals for themselves and strive to achieve them. Education propels our youth in a straight direction. Today, our youth can learn and tomorrow apply their knowledge leading by example for others to repeat the process. They learn the true meaning of "give without expectation and receive without resistance." Impartation of education is a "give-and-take" process. Education that encompasses all walks of life is transferred from one generation to another. So, if the present generation is appropriately educated and instructed, the coming one is certain to be even more properly educated and empowered to apply their knowledge.

Change for a better future again is the responsibility for every one of us. As adults, each community has a moral responsibility to own their roles and duties while coming together in an interdependent way to be the example for our youth. Tomorrow's leaders are a product of the process through example. They learn from what they observe in others who they relate to and trust and who are aligned to their purpose and values. Applied knowledge works from example and not when it is done for you. Show up as an educator or someone that empowers others to be consistent with behavior, communication, and action to be the example for tomorrow's leaders.

Introduction

By Rosalyn Kahn

I originally wrote *A Message for Tomorrow's Leaders* as a tool to motivate and inspire today's diverse youth to stay in school. People were going to speak with students in my classroom. Once the pandemic came about, the idea grew into videos that answered four questions: a person's name, occupation, a message to inspire high school and college students to stay in school, comments on the pandemic and thoughts on the protest.

I recall the day Columbine hit and school violence erupted. I lived through the violence when students went on a shooting spree at Santa Monica College. I became a faculty on watch when I reported unusual behavior on behalf of one of my students, which put my life at risk. I endured international exposure simply to help students learn the importance of timeliness.

Years ago, the Faculty Association of California Community Colleges awarded me the Part Time Faculty of the Year honor for working to get a measure on the ballot to protect teacher's rights. I received the award, but the ballot measures failed. I used to teach many classes but now I have just two. Last term, the Academic Senate wanted to find a way to secure the graduation and retention of their minority students. As part of the Communications faculty, I wanted to get a diverse group of community and business leaders to share their stories.

Once the pandemic entered the equation, the question shifted and as history unfolded. So did the stories.

I am a person who thrives on human interaction. Tears began to flow when I knew I would only see my students again on a Zoom call. No semester potlucks and sad goodbyes, just a screen shutting down saying end your meeting as the Zoom ended. I am not a fan of technology. What took hours to do now takes more hours and the work is still not done.

Yet, I also have an internal drive with a story to tell. What is happening and how do we tell the stories for those to know the other side? This was one of my best semesters with the best speeches. How can I ask others their views without sharing my own?

My name is Rosalyn Kahn. I am a professor, author, and business owner. My message to students is that this moment will go down in history. We have two choices: to celebrate or stagnate. It is a time to slow down, smell the roses, and learn for learning's sake. You can take what you learn and be better prepared for the world to come. The adjustments you make today will be minor compared to what you will face in your life. If we look at time as a precious gift that improves with each day, we will be fine.

I believe the pandemic happened as a way for the powers that be to change the landscape of our land, to make room and take out those extra few.

I read an article in an Australian newspaper that said it was all a big mistake and the entire population of the world has damaged its economy, left a lot of people out of work, and caused grave alarm to the emotional stability of so many people from domestic abuse, spousal abuse, child abuse, drug abuse and mayhem for many of the criminal mindset.

The protesters have a right to display their frustration. The deaths of so many African Americans, one after another, is not a happy part of our American past, but the needless disruption does not make things right.

We learned as youth two wrongs don't make a right. There is a means and method for dialog, I understand wholeheartedly these options have not come to pass. WE must work to learn to bring all races and humanity together through the philosophies of Martin Luther King, Mother Theresa, and Princess Diana.

Dedication

This book is dedicated to the Academic Senate of the California Community Colleges, who presented a challenge pre-pandemic: What methods can we find to maintain the minority students and help them complete their degree and move onto a four-year school?

Life as a part-time professor takes an interesting twist when you have freedom and flexibility and uncertainty. You make friends, lose friends, and then reconnect. This book is a compilation of relationships of people who have intersected with my path along the way.

Thanks to the Academic Senate member Mike Kalustian. Thanks to all the old colleagues from inside and outside my school who rose to support me from VP of Student Services: Will Marmelejo and Dr. Bradford at Pierce, who formerly worked at LACC, Dean Barbara Anderson, who attended graduate school and saw the vision, Speech chair of Pierce College Yeprem P. Davoodian, the new department chair of Speech Communication, Sarah Crachiolo, and the counseling department at LACC who worked on student issues related to the pandemic.

Thank you to James Bobik, Marketing Director and Executive Producer, and to Dr. Maryel McKinley, Manager/Producer.

Most importantly, to my spouse, David Hyman, who allowed me to take over the kitchen table to teach my classes.

Jonathan Lightman, CAE,

Nonprofit Consultant, Legislative Advocate, Attorney

When we think about the randomness in life, it is hard not to fathom how little is under our control. It is certainly a lesson for any age, but so much more in the year 2020.

I learned this the hard way when I lost my entire pancreas, gall bladder, and spleen, along with half of my stomach and a portion of my duodenum, to a rare pancreatic tumor in 2006, the first of two cancer diagnoses.

To my friends, family, colleagues, as well to strangers I met along the way, what I experienced was devastating, something that no one should ever endure. To the family and friends of those lost to the more common form of pancreatic cancer—which in 2006, had but a six percent survival rate—I basically won the genetic lottery. To them, it was inconsequential how chronically disrupted my life had become; the only thing that mattered was that I survived.

One group saw me as unlucky, another, as indescribably lucky. It all boiled down to perspective.

Frankly, perspective is the only thing we can control, through thick and thin. While we do not get to choose the times we live in, the global situation, or our genetic disposition, we can—within reasonable limits—make the best of what we have and in turn, leave the world a better place.

With that in mind, here are a few thoughts I would like to share with tomorrow's leaders.

First, the world does not revolve around us. It never has and never will. We are part of a larger social, environmental, and cultural ecosystem that requires our participation and engagement. When we take time each day, each week, and each month to invest in ourselves, our families, and our communities, however we define them, we make the world a better place.

Second, the best societal investment is to provide opportunities for both formal education and lifelong learning. Both are important and neither substitutes for the other. As much as I believe in the value of degrees and certificates, our need to continually learn without formal recognition is just as, if not more, significant.

Third, intelligence is often mistaken for wisdom and that is a tragic error. History is replete with examples of tyrants possessing fancy degrees, including those from prestigious universities, who have no compassion, judgment, or common sense, let alone the ability to write or speak. By the same token, we have all likely met people who were either denied or rejected the opportunity to attend college or attain a degree but still possess the wisdom of the ages. We do need intelligence—that is undisputable—but more importantly, we need wisdom.

Finally, resilience beats talent every single time. Life is never about how many times we are knocked down, but how often we get up. I rejected the opportunity to take a disability retirement after my pancreatic surgery because I felt I could get up again. Following my doctor's advice of doing as much as I can for as long as I can, but not so much that it would physically harm me, I continued to lead a premiere professional association of California Community College faculty for 12 years after my surgery, until my body told me I had to stop; at that point, it had enough. Even without the job, my body is still knocking me down—all the time—and as far as I am concerned, I am still getting up, however I can.

We all have challenges, some harsher than others. From whatever place we find ourselves, let us adopt as hopeful a perspective as possible and do our part to make this world a better place.

Caitlin Chen,

Home Loan Specialist,

Toastmaster

Education is important not only on an individual level, but as a productive member of society. It is a bridge for us to communicate effectively with people from all walks of life and to be able to compete in the global marketplace.

We also live in a democratic society. That means we must make choices. To make the right choices, we need to be knowledgeable in terms of this global pandemic. I think it's brought out the strength and resilience of human beings not only here in the United States, but all around the world. It shows how strong we are.

I found that one of the most important characteristics during a time of crisis is the ability to adapt. Nothing will stay the same in life. The most important thing is to be able to adapt and do it with a smile on our faces.

Knock Smith, Coach Knock, Fitness and Sports Training, First Speaker at Amino Ralph Bunch High School

This is a special hello, and best wishes to all the students at Amino Ralph Bunch High School, and LA City College, I know it's been challenging not being able to attend school and interact with your classmates, teachers, and counselors, but you guys did an awesome job of staying in focus, keeping your poise and integrity.

As you approach the end of the school year, Rosalyn has kept me up to date weekly on the progress all you students are making online with your classes, and how well you are doing in your communities.

Keep up the good work. Always help others and look out for others. Treat others with respect, love each other. There are always ways to help others, such as looking out for them and treating them with respect.

Your teachers, counselors, parents, guardians are doing an excellent job of giving you real love. I want you to pass that love on to someone else and impact your community in a positive way. You guys take care and best wishes in finishing up the school year.

Paul Hunt,
Real Estate Broker,
General Contractor, Attorney

Seems like a lot.

When I was in high school, a friend of mine once said, "Why should I learn something when I can hire somebody that already spent the time to learn it?"

My response, "How do you know that they're telling you the best advice? How do you know they're charging you fairly for that advice, and every time you need advice you need to pay them again?"

On current events and the pandemic, numbers can be twisted in any way a person wants. I think we can all agree that the pandemic does exist, it's not something we want, and it can be deadly.

I don't know why they figured that Target could use precautions, but small stores had to cut down way too much, which cut out way too many jobs. Now that we are moving towards recovery, I think we can move ahead with reasonable precautions, unless of course people who do not believe they can be contagious or people who become too lax over time increase the spread and force the government to do another broad shutdown.

On the protests, time, place, and manner count but first amendment speech is always welcome, always good. However, the message is getting too diluted.

The real problem is that a police officer does not need any actual degree to get the job. He then has training in cop shop for less than a barber has, and then is taught that his first contact with a citizen should show his supremacy and his power over that person. If the person is unfair, not taking into consideration that some people, even an innocent person, may find it offensive and may resist and the next time people contact police, they fear that behavior.

Then if there's a cop that has a claim against them and it is investigated by the same guy that has barbecues with the cop on the weekend, we have a problem that needs to be solved. However, as each different group wants to bring in their causes and their separate demands, I think it takes us away from the main issue of letting the good cops become great cops, and to not make it easy to be a bad cop. Let's keep the message straight on certain reforms that are needed, rather than all the other issues. Thank you very much for your time. I hope this helps your class.

Kat Haber,

Pandemic Survivor,

TEDx organizer

Being the first carries with it excitement, adventure, and deep personal growth.

Being among the first female cadets at the United States Air Force Academy helped me grow an internal grit and discipline that served well later in my life.

To qualify for the first aerial female ski freestyle spot in the Calgary Olympics in 1988, I discovered physical risk and the power of consistent training.

I founded a virtual Rotary Club focused on "creating a more peaceful world" when there were very few females in Rotary which continues to build bridges internationally.

I walked across the United States in the Great March for Climate Action speaking and listening to Americans who both understood science and those who doubted humans could impact God's creation. Be the first at something you love. Tomorrow's women leaders will thank you for the shoulders upon which they stand.

The pandemic virus is an ever-morphing set of physical symptoms. Imagine putting each one on the face of a die. Put several dice in a Yahtzee cup. Shake well. Toss them out on the table. My body is a daily morph calling me to constantly pay attention to and build up my immune system. I remain in quiet isolation healing my body and dealing with the way humans might live in peace and in harmony in the elements of our places.

This pandemic pause provides me quiet to rethink my living in E*arth*'s fragile living systems. This year we lost four million acres to wildfires in California and caused fires in the Amazon, the lungs of Earth that balances our water and oxygen cycles globally. I have removed the insurance from my car and not driven or flown for nine months.

TEDxVail hosted 29 conversations themed: "pause...Countdown Pandemic Clues, Climate Acts, Local Impacts" with elders, youth, CEO's, NGO local leaders. Clues for you:

1. Use less, be more.

2. Here is where it's from.

3. Now, now, now time is on our side during this climate emergency.

4. Ask questions to learn.

5. Ever listen.

6. Precautionary principle.

7. We are enough.

8. We don't count polar bears in parts per million.

9. Flatten the curves of the pandemic and climate.

10. We belong to each other.

Monte Perez,

President of

Los Angeles Mission College

I've been president of Los Angeles Mission College for 10 years and have had nothing but a good time here. I've enjoyed every minute and particularly enjoyed the students and the faculty and the staff here. Mission College is probably the most beautiful campus in all the nine Los Angeles community college campuses.

I'm writing this for Professor Kahn and for the Communication 101 class. What I see in students that have been emailing me and in our enrollments is one and one thing only: You are committed to making sure you finish your education and move on to your goals and careers and to higher education.

Our enrollments are as strong as ever. If we compare our enrollment this year to last year, we're above. This pandemic has taken a toll, but it hasn't changed your dedication to finish your education and to move on and return to your communities and society and contribute in ways that will benefit and support each other.

What are my feelings with this virus? It is a huge test, huge challenge. We can step up, address it, and overcome it. There are still a lot of unknowns and we're still learning about it. We're in stage Two now in Los Angeles County.

Stage Three is when we can operate more fully in person. We will plan for that time. This summer we offered virtual online education in all our classes, but in the fall, we will offer some classes in person, mostly in labs and activity courses and career technical education that requires hands on. We'll do it in a safe, healthy way, following guidance by the state of California and LA County Public Health.

More important, what I see is you students have great character, tremendous resilience, and care about people. That's why you're doing your best to wear your masks in public, to protect others as well as protect yourself. I know you're dedicated to your families, your loved ones, to your community, and want to keep us all on track to full recovery. There will be challenges of course. We still have health and safety challenges and economic challenges. When I talk about resilience, I'm talking about you being able to recover completely, economically, academically, emotionally, and socially.

My hat's off to you. Nothing but compliments to communications class Professor Kahn. Each of you can feel free to contact us. We have all the support services necessary. If you go online and look at our website and get into the Student Support Services website, you'll see all the services where you'll get immediate assistance. Summer is here, and I wish you all a good summer. I believe our futures are bright. We need to keep together, be steadfast, and remember we're Eagles strong.

Jessica Jaffe,

Precision Chiropractic

It is okay to not know what you want to do in school. Don't be afraid to try things you think you might be interested in and fail and try again. Take time off school if you need to but never stop learning. Trades and working in those fields are valuable and not to be looked down on. Don't be afraid to fail. Once you're at the bottom, you can only go up.

Take care of your health, eat well, drink water, exercise and meditate and don't give in to fear. Fear makes us unhealthy.

Everyone has a right to speak their mind and be respectful to everyone, including those with different opinions. Keep it civil. There's no need for violence. We should be able to tolerate each other.

Brooke Hennon,

Head of Customer Success

What you do now will paint your path for tomorrow. The pandemic is very scary and real. Sadly, it is a marathon, not a sprint. We are in the second act. The true test will come as people think we are coming back for air. Be vigilant, mindful, and aware of your needs.

Natalia Korol,

Director, Producer

Here is my thinking about this situation. Number one would be to say human life matters. Doesn't matter who you are, black, white, Latino, Asian, you are a human being. Nobody cares if you are Muslim, Jewish, Christian, Buddhist, we all have the same color blood. We need to work together, not fight each other. We must visit each other. Let's stay together and be happy and enjoy our life. This will take thought.

I am an event coordinator and producer of the show *Perfect Lady and Perfect Gentleman*. And I also publish a magazine, *Hollywood People Magazine*.

What do you think about the education? A good question. It's important for our children to have a good education, first at home. But that's not enough. Our children need to go to school, where they have good instructors who can teach them and where they create friendships with other children. Education is important to the future of this country.

With the pandemic all around us, just be safe. Stay at home. If it's possible, wash your hands and be happy and healthy.

Nicole Younesi,
Noelle's Fashions
Marketing Director

I am the marketing manager at my parents' business, Noelle's, in downtown Los Angeles. Unfortunately, due to the pandemic, we have been closed for the past month. However, we stay positive and optimistic through these difficult times with music, exercise, and daily gratitude. Whether that's through prayer, exercising, going outside, going on hikes, or spending time with family, keeping positive is the most important thing to do during this time.

Write down little tasks you can complete, whether it's minimal tasks you can do at home or reaching out to old friends or old family who you probably haven't made enough time for. These little things keep morale up.

Also important is staying healthy, whether it's through a good diet or staying hydrated by drinking warm liquids. It's important.

Rosalyn Kahn, who was my speech professor at SMC back in 2010, recently reached out to me to make this video. I hope that you guys take everything that she teaches you and apply it in your life.

One of those things for me was speech, which gave me the confidence to speak in public. I use that skill in my everyday life and I also use it in business. It's important to have the confidence to speak your truth in front of others and to spread awareness of what's happening nowadays.

If you have social media platforms, make sure you relay a message to your small or large audience and tell them how they can help, whether by wearing masks or gloves when they go out to the house or by diet and exercise. All those things are rewarding.

Pepper Jay,
Music Producer

Hi, I'm Pepper Jay giving a big shout out to Rosalyn Kahn, author of *Dogs and Roses*. Her book is helpful when it comes to relieving stress and anxiety.

Rosalyn asked me to speak to you about why it's important to stay in school. I have a lifetime teaching credential with the State of California. I taught a lot of junior high or what they call now Middle School, and in some places high school, college. So here are my thoughts.

There are two reasons to stay in school.

When I say stay in school, I mean to graduate from high school and go forward with advanced schooling. The first reason is that when you want to do something in life that requires training or a certificate or diploma, you go to that school and you achieve the steps required to fulfill your dream. Whether you want to be a teacher, a doctor, a lawyer, perhaps you want to own a business, whatever it is, you might go to a two- or four-year university.

You want to be a mechanic, an electrician, computer engineer, computer scientist, or nursing, whatever it is, maybe it's a trade school you want to go to. Figure out what you want to do, then use the school to complete whatever the basic steps are for you to be able to do what you want to do to achieve your dreams.

The second reason to stay in school is quite the opposite, even when you have no idea what you want to do, even if you have some interests but you can't see how they might turn into making a living and you are lost.

Stay in school. It's a safe space. Once you're out in the world, you're responsible for putting a roof over your head and food on your table. When you're in school, when you don't know what you want to do, two things happen. First, you learn about different things and you think, "Oh, yeah, I never thought that maybe I'd be interested in that."

This will give you a lead as to what you want to do. It'll keep you safe off the streets. It'll keep you out of jail because you won't get into trouble while you're trying to figure it out.

You finish high school. Okay, so you have a diploma. Good. Or you go to a two-year junior college or community college. You get basic stuff. This buys you time to figure out your goals. Stay in school.

Rita Boccuzzi,

Financial Consultant, Coach, Speaker

I love inspiring people with taking a holistic approach to life, focusing on bettering our mindsets through self-development, preservation of what's good in the world, and creating perseverance in our lives so that we can all be prosperous.

Many challenges have come up in this past year 2020. We can look at those challenges as a place to create an opportunity for us to overcome and help others do the same. Start with controlling our attitude and our activities.

With a pandemic, I would ask, "Where is your focus?"

I know in my world, I love focusing on the opportunity, yet I see so many people focusing on the crisis. I like to shift that focus to focusing on the opportunity of being patient with others and yourself, showing love by wearing masks to protect others and focus on what is certain in our lives, or create certainty for ourselves and others.

As far as the protests go, I believe we should voice our opinions to stop perpetuating racism in the world. But I want to do so mindfully. I want to validate and verify the groups that I'm part of. I want to make sure I'm not being conditioned and I'm following my criteria. Do the same.

Here too, we need to be mindful of others because sometimes people might be silent because they're dealing with too much pain or they're praying for all of us. Einstein has an amazing quote: Problems cannot be solved at the level of consciousness where they were created.

I believe that as we get educated around all our facts, an educated society becomes an elevated society, which changes the path to freedom for all of us. You get to create that right now for future generations.

Ask yourself empowering questions. What would you love to do? Am I open to receiving the wisdom that I can partner to do good, be good and make good in the world so that all we can all flourish together?

Stacia Belyeu,

Nurse

I'm a registered nurse with a 25-year career in the Air Force reserves as a flight nurse. I knew early on that I wanted to be a registered nurse. I went into the Air Force about 15 years after becoming a nurse because I was looking down the line at retirement for a way for me to do a different type of nursing and look out for my future.

I would like to say to any young students out there, do what you must do now, so you will be able to do what you want to do down the line. Essentially, that means stay in school, study hard, do the best you can, get your degree and then down the line, you'll be able to do whatever it is you want to do.

Dr. Todd Binkley,

DrWellness

I am a Doctor of Chiropractic and practitioner of functional medicine. Rosalyn asked me to send a message for you this morning.

Functional Medicine means that I use standard blood tests to identify conditions early enough that you can often fix them with food supplements and exercise.

My message to everyone during this global pandemic is that among other things, it is evidence of widespread functional immunodeficiency. It's a very infectious and dangerous virus and that's why it's a pandemic. But it's also easy to kill since 97% of the people that end up in the hospital survive this virus.

If you pay any attention to the news at all, you'll know the people who are most vulnerable to it are older people, people who are obese, people who have diabetes, and people who have poor health and poor health care.

Given all of that, one simple thing everyone can do is to maximize your body's immune system with one simple vitamin and that is vitamin D. The standard government recommendations for vitamin D vary between 1,000 and 2,000 units a day. These recommendations are designed to prevent rickets and reduce your risk of osteoporosis, but they will not be sufficient to keep your immune system strong.

Thousands of practitioners of functional medicine around the country have witnessed dramatic reductions in the incidence, prevalence, and severity of respiratory infections of all types if people take adequate amounts of vitamin D, defined by blood tests that determine whether your immune system is getting what it needs to function efficiently. Most people, but not everyone, can take 5,000 units of vitamin D per day. Thin women who weigh less than 120 pounds might achieve sufficient blood levels on 4,000 units a day. Anyone who has not been taking 5,000 units of vitamin D per day for several months is better off taking 10,000 units a day for two to three months at least until this global pandemic passes. Best wishes everyone will all get through this eventually. Live long.

Tony V., From England

I'm a friend of Rosalyn, who I met when I was traveling in Los Angeles in February 2020. She asked me to send my thoughts and observations on what's happening in terms of the race riots in America.

Obviously, there were some issues recently in London, with the Black Lives Matter protests, and obviously with what happened to that gentleman in Minnesota, and the different video viewpoints. I don't think you have to be a genius to realize that was horrific, sad, and endemic.

Let me word this correctly. I think it's sad the way the world is now. We are in the middle of a global pandemic, as you know, and lots of people's lives have been changed for good or for better. A new normal will happen in terms of shopping and in terms of socializing in general. I'm outside a place in London where my girlfriend's having a scan. I'd usually go in with her, but I can't because of what's going on.

You get to talk to me in my Mini. We have to accept the things and survive and thrive or we can get caught up in what's happening in the moment in terms of life and look at the negative or we can try and see the positive now.

I don't think I can see any positivity in what happened to that gentleman, and how he died, and the circumstances around how he died. A lot of people have taken up the banner of Black Lives Matter and will protest.

The problem is the minority of people within that protest group who don't want it to be peaceful. They want it to be issues and problems and violence because they're unhappy with everything else that's going on. This is their outlet. This is their way of getting it out.

It's the same here in a UK. There are people that want to protest peacefully and want to give black people a voice, which is 100% required, needed and overdue. There are also people who are in chaos, who want to see the world burn. I don't know why.

They're the same people that as soon as they hear maybe the Chinese are responsible for something, they hate all Chinese people and Chinese food. And when they hear about Corona, they'll boycott and want to ban the beer. There it is, in my mind. That's the technical term, morons, losers, whatever you want to call them. I'm guessing that the whole world hasn't missed a day.

I think if you take a little bit of timeout, my best advice is what I've taught everybody, take time to read between the lines.

What are people? What is influencing you now? If it's Facebook, if it's Twitter, if it's the Internet, if it's your friends, they influenced you. They were natural. We're humans, we are influenced by people around us. So how do they influence you? Are they convincing you that there's a global conspiracy of 5g networks about to burn you down? Or are they saying, isn't it wonderful that there's not much air traffic in the world? The skies are clear, and trees are beautiful and stuff like that, which is tangible, right?

Focus on what you can see and feel and what's tangible, rather than stories. That's probably the biggest thing now.

Think back on what you know, what you want out of your life. If your focus in life is to be happy and successful, and success equals happiness in my mind, then focus on that. Nothing else should be around you except happiness. You hear all these wonderful things happen, happiness is a state of mind, a skill that we were all born with, that we tend to lose over time, that we spend the rest of our lives trying to find again.

Because we were happy as children and we just loved, we ate food, we slept great. Look how we do that now. You know, so I leave you with that.

If you want to contact me or reach out on Instagram, Ants 1701. I always respond. Message me and say who you are. You saw this and you want to talk and I'm happy to talk or send you a postcard from England. Be safe, be well and be happy.

Victoria Morgan,

Family Law Attorney

I'm a family law attorney in Ventura, California. Here's why I think you should stay in school even when you can make more money.

As soon as I got my education, I went to my boss and said, "Hey, I heard I can make more money for getting an education. I got it. Now, let's see it."

I got a big fat raise, which was awesome. Second reason is that it's hard to go back to school later in life, and you might change your mind, decide you want an education later, decide that you want to get out of the trade that you're in and do something different. It requires an education to do that. It's hard to go back.

Third, once you get your education, it's yours forever. Nobody can take it away.

We have seen all these riots and such going on recently. That's not the way to make change. The way to make change is to know who to go to and to know how to use the processes that are afforded us in this country. We have a constitution that allows us to make change to the country.

These people who are rioting are not using the correct processes, and they're never going to get what they're asking for. But if you're educated, and you go in and you do it the right way, that's how you really make change.

Stay in school, get yourself an education, and make the change that you want to see in this country.

Wyn Robertson,

Electrical Engineer

Rosalyn asked me to tell you a little bit about myself as far as my occupation goes and my reaction to the pandemic. I'm an electronic engineer and graduated from Cal Poly in 1987. I've had more than 30 years in my career, which had its ups and downs, working in Silicon Valley, I got laid off a few times here and there.

That taught me to always live off less than I make and put a little aside so when the hard times hit there'll be some money there. Over the long run, it's been a good career.

As far as schooling, learn math and physics. I dreaded physics at first, but it turned out to be a lot of fun.

I took a lot of math and a lot of engineering classes. When you get out into your career, you need to learn a whole new way to do things, but it's been rewarding working on interesting projects and medical products and lasers and all different kinds of stuff. If you're interested and you have a feel for it, go for engineering. If you don't think engineering is the thing for you, it probably won't be. If you do, then I'd say go for it and work hard. It's challenging and rewarding.

I've been retired but do consulting. With the pandemic, the consulting has dried up so I'm doing the shutdown at home like everybody else and trying to keep the family together and occupy myself. Nobody I know has it but we're still careful to wear a mask when we go to Costco and minimize our trips out. I still go up on the bike trail to ride my bike or go running or whatever. Stay safe and take care out there and stay in school. Do it to find what you enjoy doing and go for it.

Lee Pound,

Speaker, Book Editor and Designer, Workshop Leader

As a book editor and writing workshop leader, I train people to write and publish books. Over the years I've edited and published over 20 books for clients, including two ghost-written books.

Rosalyn asked me to comment on my profession, on the pandemic and on protests. I believe all three depend on each other. Writing gives everyone a powerful way to express their opinions and to research and understand the truth about problems we face in the United States today.

For students, stay in school. You will not only get the skills you need to compete in today's economy, but you will also learn powerful research and logic skills that will help you understand the conflicts evident in today's world. Without education, much of what happens in the world today makes no sense, so people go with what their elders told them when they are young.

Understanding the pandemic takes more than listening to your favorite news show. Disease is a medical problem, not a political problem. All actions must be based on the science of medicine and on rigorous research and testing. Use the critical skills gained through education to understand the problems we face today.

In my work as a writer and family historian, my primary emphasis is to use the proven facts of the matter when deciding which position to take. Leave emotion out of it, act in a responsible manner.

Protest is a great example. People in different classes and areas of the country have different experiences. We as Americans have a basic right to protest actions taken by our government and private companies that affect us in adverse ways. Use that right wisely.

Yeprem Davoodian, Department Chair, Communication Studies, Pierce College

I am also the Honors Director for the Honors Transfer program here at Pierce College. A few motivational words for our students would be to try new things. If you step out of your comfort zone, that's where you learn. It's not whether you're successful or you fail. It's about learning through your experiences. We learn new things, new pathways open, and we're better able to guide ourselves through education and life.

Some thoughts on the pandemic. It has been tough for everyone, staff, faculty, and our students, especially our students. In this unprecedented time where things are new, things shift and change.

There are uncertainties, but keep in mind that as a human race, we have persevered over trauma and tragedy, and we will overcome this obstacle as well.

With that being said, I wish everyone a healthy life.

Frank Grant, Business Owner/ Automotive Technician and Mechanic

Please do well in school.

You'll need to pass the knowledge and experience you've gained on to as many people as possible. Make yourself a valuable individual for future employment or becoming a successful entrepreneur.

To solve, for example, Black Lives Matter, a small revolution or large-scale protests need to happen. It's true that history repeats itself although it's proven that with enough well-organized protesting positive changes are inevitable.

You do not want to fall in the category of Drop-Dead Stupid. You cannot babysit the world. However, you have the knowledge and fortitude to set an example for everyone around you. By wearing an effective mask and protecting your eyes as needed, the pandemic numbers will go down. Stay strong and think twice if necessary. One or more wrong moves could possibly cost you your life and others around you.

Alma Dang,

Preschool Teacher and Ms. Latina Global

I was born in Mexico, a land with beautiful beaches and a rich culture. That includes traditional cuisine, hand-crafted artwork, and ancient architecture.

I moved to San Diego, California 39 years ago to begin a new adventure. Although I had a college degree in education and was a preschool teacher, I decided to change my career. I'm currently an Investor and Realtor.

I was crowned Miss Maeya in 2018 at the Universe Multicultural Film Festival and Mrs. Tourism Mexico USA in Portland, Oregon.

I also won the award Beauty for a Cause, Best National Costume in Mexico 2019, and Mrs. Latina Global California 2018-2019.

We filmed the video for a television commercial for the Cancer Hope Village in Chiang Mai and for LBM Academy in San Diego, California.

I modeled in various fashion shows in San Diego, Hollywood, and Los Angeles. I'm one of the models for the Victoria Guadron Cosmetic Line in USA.

I strongly believe in giving back to my community, so I have volunteered at St. Vincent de Paul Medical Clinic in San Diego, California for the homeless. I'm Founder President and CEO of my own organization, Alma's Angel Care, a non-profit organization helping kids stay healthy through soccer and studying.

My mission is to raise my voice and provide the necessary help needed to fully support less fortunate kids to successfully continue their education both mentally, physically, and spiritually.

In my spare time I enjoy belly dancing, Mexican regional dance, golf, playing piano, acting and CrossFit.

To students: You are born to make your dreams come true. Never give up and always remember books are one of your best friends.

The pandemic offers the opportunity for people to change mentally, physically, emotionally, and spiritually.

Angeline Benjamin,
High Impact Coach with Results, Motivational Speaker, Author

Find somebody (a mentor) who will help you stay motivated and support you to move forward, especially now that there are programs offered by people who want to help others through online tutoring programs and mentoring programs.

Plenty of people want to help you. The key is, do you want the help? This is a two-way street. As a student, you must act and take responsibility for your life.

I can say this from my own experience. I came to this country when I was 18 years old with my younger sister, unable to speak English. I didn't have any relatives or friends. But I had a plan. I had several support systems from my parents who loved me unconditionally, my sisters and brothers who are my cheerleaders, my teachers who were there to teach, mentor and help me, my friends who were willing to help me, a mentor who motivated me. All I did was to show up, ask, act, and take responsibility for my actions.

It's up to you. Surround yourself with can do and positive attitude people. You will go through ups and downs through life, but if you stay motivated and have determination, and most importantly have a mentor who sincerely wants to help, you will get through this.

Life is full of valleys and hills. Some of us are in the valley and some of us are already up on the hills. I will leave you with this motivational quote from Nora Roberts: "If you don't go after what you want, you'll never have it. If you don't ask, the answer is always NO. If you don't step forward, you are always in the same place."

We can't live in fear. Being a scientist (a microbiologist), I learned viruses will always be around, one disappears, others appear, or reappear with different DNA or RNA structures. They will not disappear! Viruses are opportunists (like parasites) once they multiply in our bodies! The most important lesson I learned to prevent the spread of the virus is to practice good personal hygiene and sanitation and build your immune system by staying healthy. Believe it or not, hand washing is one of the easiest ways to remove the virus from your hands (since we use our hands to touch so many things).

Viruses do not multiply outside the human body (unlike bacteria)! Every year, we have a flu season, this one of course is a lot more contagious than others, but the prevention method is the same. Because our body can fight the virus by building antibodies, staying healthy should be a priority, especially now.

Is it easy? Definitely no. We need to be diligent and have common sense. To stay healthy is a work in progress. During this pandemic, I learned we need to have an open mind to learn new things that we did not feel comfortable doing. Having a positive and can-do attitude I believe is important during this pandemic. We should not surround our life with fear. Instead, find a solution on how to stay healthier, have a positive mindset, get involved.

Staying at home, locking ourselves up, and not staying active does not help our mind and body to stay healthy. I learned to do more online, be active virtually, learn new things and yet I still go outside for a walk, a hike, do my grocery, and other shopping. Even do safe travelling!

I have learned to be adaptable and flexible. I have always avoided in the past eating or staying at unsanitary places. Now it is more important to do so.

What happens if we get the virus and get sick? If we are healthy, we will recover! Just like in the past when I got the flu, I built my immune system and I recovered. During flu season I did not hug everybody and always washed my hands thoroughly after I shook hands with others, so why should this time be any different?

In fact, I became more diligent now. Why? It is a long flu season! It is called a pandemic because it happened all over the world at the same time. It is a larger scale of flu season and throughout the world.

As a person, I have always looked at the positive first rather than the negative. Because of this pandemic, I am hoping all of us will put a priority on good personal hygiene, cleanliness, sanitation, and health as a basic requirement in life and focus on prevention rather than reaction. Before, some people were not taking seriously basic health safety like practicing good personal hygiene, cleanliness, sanitation, contamination, etc.

I hope this pandemic will teach us the importance of practicing these habits. So, in the end, we will protect our parents, grandparents. Many elderly (60+) people with underlying health issues, etc. died from this flu, which before has always been my concern.

Candace Mae Gruber,

Business Owner

Good day. I am the owner of a small business in Southern California and I was asked to create this message for the leaders of tomorrow.

I am a leadership consultant, trainer and coach and a public speaker. Today I want to motivate you as a student, whether in high school or college, to be excited about the opportunity to grow. While you're in school, please don't just look at the hard skills you're learning. Stretch your mind, get out of your comfort zone, become your best self. That's going to happen when you dig deep into these questions: Why are you in school? Why are you in college? What do you want to contribute to this world?

You're taking up space here and your life is a dash. If you look at a tombstone, you're born, and you die. That little dash in between is your entire life.

While you're young, it seems like you have a whole lifetime ahead of you that seems to stretch a long, long time. But the older you get, the faster those years go. Suddenly, you're looking back on your life wondering, where did the years go? I got up. I went to school, I came home went to work. I did a routine. I didn't really give any thought into anything I was doing. I did what my parents told me to do. I went to work, and I showed up. I did what my boss told me to do.

But what do you want to do if you dig deep down into your soul? What is it that you want to do? What are your passions? What are your dreams? What are your hopes? Do you know what you're good at? Are you good at relating to people? Are you good at processing things in detail? Are you good at creating? We all have the power of creation, but some of us are more creative than others. Some of us are good at influencing others.

I know what your strengths are. Focus on your strength areas, become your best self. Surround yourself with people who have expertise in the areas where your weaknesses are, let that be their strength and pull them into you so that together, you make yourself a stronger team. Don't try to be the head of the class all the time. Surround yourself with other people who are even smarter than you because they will lift you up as you lift down others. You want to be lifted up.

If you're always the one talking, there's no room for growth. Create a balance, strive to figure out what your values are in life and what those values look like every day. If you value people, what are you doing every day to say you value people? If you value family, how are you interacting with your family. These answers are the core of life. This is the character that you develop. And when you develop who you are on the inside, and you become attuned to who you are on the inside, then you're ready to start working with other people on the outside.

I challenge you with that. I encourage you that while you're in school, it's a beautiful time. We have for faculty, a fourth intelligence, we have physical intelligence, emotional intelligence, which is even higher than intellectual intelligence. We have spiritual intelligence. I challenge you to look at all four of those intellects and use them.

We have the five senses that you learned in elementary school, taste, touch, hearing, sight, and feeling. Beyond those we have six faculties, memory, reason, perception, imagination, intuition and will. When you tap into those six faculties, you can make a difference in the world. You will create and manifest things of great power. I hope that motivates you.

Mari-lin Harris,

Kindness Coach, Hypnotherapist, Producer of Kindness Matters Conferences

Stay in school, you will feel better about yourself. Keep feeling good about yourself.

Repeat to yourself, "I am enough!"

The Pandemic is a great time to pivot to change your life. Start a side business for yourself to help other people.

Protests: If you feel called to do so - follow your own institution. With issues or challenges that you are faced with you could also pick an organization to volunteer for.

Robbie Motter,

Founder, Global Society for Female Entrepreneurs

I am the CEO and founder of the Global society for Female Entrepreneurs, whose mission is to inspire, empower, mentor, educate, and connect women so they become successful entrepreneurs and enjoy a fulfilling, productive and abundant life.

I think going to school is positive because there's so much to learn. You can figure out what you're going to do for the rest of your life and become an expert in that field. You get to meet people that eventually will go on and do other things that will always be there for you to reconnect with.

They can always be of help to you as you grow and move on in your career. It's important to stay in school, go to college, finish high school, and sit down and decide what you want to be and then become the best that you can be in that profession.

The pandemic has had a lot of impact on many people. I think it's also allowed people to rethink what they are doing. Is it really their passion? What else could they do? How can they add new things?

I've heard many people say that during the pandemic they made more money than before, maybe because they were more focused. They weren't running in a million places. They had more time to think. It's been a terrible thing. But I do think in many ways, it's also been a good thing, not the pandemic itself, but the time that people are with family more, to be together to contact people they haven't seen and talked to for a long time.

Sometimes we just get so busy that we bypass the little things that mean a lot. I think from this pandemic much has been learned, as well as we've learned to be careful, wash our hands, wear a mask, and keep the six-foot separation. We learn so much more. So that really is my opinion on the pandemic.

My opinion on the protest: I believe people can protest in a respectable and honest manner, not in a manner where they destroy buildings and burn buildings and beat people up. I don't think that that helps them to get what they're trying to accomplish.

I think you sit down and talk about the issues so they can be worked out. Tearing up buildings and putting small businesses out of business to me is not the answer. So hopefully we can have more peaceful protests and all these terrible protests where there are fires and beat ups and burnings and killing people will stop.

Carmelita Pittman,

Founder, Rose Breast Cancer Society, Singer, Radio Show Host

I am a former Los Angeles Unified art educator of many years. I have graduated from the classroom and now the world is my classroom because my organization, the Rose Breast Cancer Society, is a living memorial for my mother who put me through USC on a secretary's salary. It is my way of giving back to the community in her memory. It is my labor of love.

As a former educator, I want to encourage all young people out there who hear my voice to take education seriously, because knowledge is power. When you have knowledge because of education, it puts you far ahead of the game and sometimes life appears to be a game. But as you know, it's not always easy, especially now during these times of pandemic.

I recommend that everybody follow the science. Listen to the experts who know what they're talking about and cover yourself with a mask so that you can protect each other. I mean, a lot of people don't believe that, but it has helped a lot. So many lives can still be saved if more and more people would do that simple little thing.

I know it's not comfortable or convenient. Right now, I'm talking without a mask, but that's because I want you to be able to see who's talking to you. Remember to wash your hands. Often if you sing Happy Birthday two times, it comes out to about 20 seconds, which is the amount of time that you should use to wash your hands. And of course, we all know that six feet apart social distancing is also valuable. The states that ignored that had a price to pay.

The pandemic has taken its toll on the number of lives that have been lost. We need to pay attention and do the right thing. And I want to encourage everybody to make the best use of this time. This pandemic might be a blessing in disguise. While you are able, those of you who can be able to pursue those things that you put off for so long, you can do it now. You can write that book, you can write that song. You can paint that painting. Speaking of painting, I've got to get busy. I've got a portrait to do. And I want to thank you for your time. And I want to thank Rosalyn Kahn for inviting me to be part of this. Stay safe.

Christopher Salem,

CRS Group Holdings LLC,

Empowered Fathers in Action, Inc.

Education is important for anyone at any age. Staying in school provides students with the discipline to commit to learning knowledge and then with experience over time to apply that knowledge to solve problems and create solutions. It's about learning how to solve problems and create solutions through the discipline of going to school.

I believe for people overall this is a golden opportunity during this pandemic to learn how to be present and go within for clarity. This is necessary to maximize their strengths aligned to their true core values. Also, this is a time for people to learn patience and gratitude with oneself and others. Give without expectation and receive without resistance.

I support people who believe in their cause so long as they do not impose their beliefs on others, interfere, and pose harm to others. Come from peace and empower people to draw their own conclusion to how they see the world and stand up for their values.

Laurie Davis,

Educator, Author, Entrepreneur, Talk Show Host

For the past 50 years I have been an educator in many different environments. When I sit with my grandson showing him how to do something or cook with my granddaughter, I realize how much the public-school system, post-secondary institutions, on stage as a keynote speaker, leading a workshop, broadcasting and finally the school of hard knocks are the many ways to accumulate an education.

In our first year of life, we learn and take in everything. If we continued to learn at that same rate throughout our lives, we would all be geniuses. It is imperative that we take advantage of every opportunity to be educated. Even when we mess up, we are learning. By nature, we are curious beings and life-long learning is as important as the air we breathe. To attend high school or university or a trade school or any other formal learning environment is a privilege and an honor. It is never going to be a burden to carry around for the rest of your life. Go for it!

When we were learning to walk, we fell. What did we do? We got back up and tried again. Then we fell and hit our heads on the coffee table. What did we do? We cried and got right back up and got it done. Now we are walking but clumsy still and fall again, skinning our knees on the pavement. What did we do? Get the picture?

School can be like that. Ups and downs, failures, and successes, but we need to remember the determination that is already within us to get things done. Learning to get back up each time we fall is instinctive until we allow others to influence us and change our minds about things. Where would we be if the first time we fell trying to walk we never got back up to see what was around the corner waiting for us?

The recent pandemic has been disruptive, disturbing, damaging, and for many devastating. I have many thoughts on many different levels about the whole thing. We have been placed in very compromising positions, emotionally, spiritually, and economically.

On the upside there have been some gifts. Parents at home spending more time with their children has been advantageous to some. People are walking more and spending time in nature. We have been reaching out to help and support our front-line workers and seniors. New life is coming to the planet with the births that are happening, and one could even expect a second baby boom on the way. We have had to become more resourceful and creative about how we can do things differently. Being grateful for the little things and appreciating what we have is enough and do we really need what we think we need? We have had time to clean, reevaluate life, pay forward, write books, and get caught up with our projects. We have also learned to live one day at a time, which is all we have anyway.

I am challenged by the protests. I believe we have a right to peacefully protest anything that is not acceptable to us. Historically we were taught that by Gandhi, Martin Luther King Jr., Nelson Mandela, Mother Theresa, and many other world leaders.

We all know that what we focus on increases. Mother Theresa once said, "I will never support an antiwar rally, but I will participate in a march for peace." The peaceful protesters after the George Floyd incident also attracted more criminals, police brutality, looting and damaging unsupervised stores and homes. These behaviors are rooted in hate and division.

There are only three keys to peace and harmony. Love, gratitude, and forgiveness are essential for people to connect and move forward. With all that is going on, our world has been completely turned upside down and will never be the same again. Perhaps that is a good thing as there are lots of things that need to be cleaned up and improved upon right now if we are to survive it all.

Health care, education, mental health services, the justice system, policing, the banking system, welfare, government, all of it needs to be revamped and changed to provide the services that we pay for every single day. These are things we need to be marching and protesting for rather than a limited view of the fact that we are all important. Those of us on the planet today were not here when history was happening that created a lot of damage that people cannot let go of. That is called unforgiveness and that is holding us all back right now. When we are walking down the street and looking behind us, we will run into something or fall or trip. As the kids would say, we are doing a lot of 'trippin' right now. We need to get over ourselves.

Jackie Goldberg,

The Pink Lady

Education is one of the things they cannot ever take away from you. Use it or lose the chance to be a free independent individual.

The pandemic is part of an ever-evolving life experience on our earth. New things come up all the time, good and bad, that make us aware that the unknown is always going to be around so we must deal with it and every other thing that happens.

It's not easy but there will always be the "Unknown Factor" for humans.

We all should have the right to protest what we consider to be 'injustice' but in a peaceful and thoughtful manner. The problem is that there are forces that are explosive and those people only want to destroy people's right to be free to "say it as it is."

No one should ever be stilled if they want to be heard. Freedom is what most of us want and we will fight for the right to have it.

Songwriting Shane,

MESSAGE OF PEACE,

Grammy Recording Artist, Multi-Award-Winning Singer/Songwriter, Retired NJ State Police Officer, was International Team Leader of CISM and 9/11 Ground Response Team in NYC, Activist in the LA Communities.

Mission: Unite all hearts for peace

Growing up,
I was taught there was only *One God and One World.*
I was taught to *respect ALL people.*

I learned that there are people who feel entitled in all walks of life, both rich and poor. But that didn't make it right.

In school I learned of the trials our Forefathers went through to unite our states in the name of brotherly love, freedom and to bring about one nation under God to always be indivisible... with liberty ... and justice for all.

I was taught to be responsible, respectful, hard-working, and thankful for all things. I still thank God for all things and pray for those who need help and healing.

That means *all people.*

What I saw during my lifetime was sometimes quite the opposite of what I was taught in school and it often saddened me. I saw division, control and discrimination by people who deemed themselves *"privileged"* or *"abused"* by their life situations.

My generation was taught at home and school to help others and *not discriminate.*

My generation followed the direction of our forefathers before us and we continued to fight for the rights of *all* people being abused by an *unjust* System, led by Abusive Leaders/Bosses/Spouses, etc.

My generation died in wars and *cried out* ***give peace a chance!!!***

Many in my generation became victims of abuse by those who were taught to blame entire Races, Nationalities or Religions for their own sad situations or bad choices life.

We have *all suffered enough!!!* We've all suffered through this discrimination and abuse running rampant throughout the years. And yet, those of us still alive from the 40s, 50s, 60s, 70s, 80s generations hold on with faith and knowledge ... as we slowly watch our country ... and so many other countries falling apart ... due to the greed and hatred of man. And *no-one listens*!

IT'S 2020 ... I am thankful to have been properly raised and educated with respect and love for others *without prejudice* and my country is still *one nation under God*. That contract, our Constitution, was signed sealed and delivered. And I thank our forefathers for their death-defying mission to achieve that goal for the betterment of life and brotherly love for the good of all.

My opinion on pandemics:

Power and greed cause havoc and wars in all nations. Germ warfare, chemical warfare, psychological warfare, monetary warfare, etc. are all the works of those who devise evil toward others. I believe they will be dealt with when they meet their Maker.

That's in almost every Bible around the world.

My advice:

Please stay in school!! That is your saving grace and key to sanity and discernment during these crises. War never brings peace. Hatred never brings unity. Discrimination doesn't solve anything. There are good and bad people in all walks of life.

Most people around the world want peace and freedom and justice, like most of us.

***Opinion on protest*:** Fighting and yelling to deaf ears isn't the answer.

Act intelligent, especially now. *Safety is a priority!*

We need good police protection. We need unity and respect of all people. Otherwise, we continue to create more victims by our own demise.

What I learned in school and at home remains the same. I'll share an educated principle of life and inner strength with you.

Every one of us knows we are here on earth for a short time. No one is in control that or anything, for that matter. We are *all* given an allotted time here to do the best we can with our lives. So, be creative, helpful, and loving towards one another and to be thankful for the world and life around you.

Peacefully and Intelligently Demand:

* Respect for God and our country as was so ordained.

* Demand honesty with zero tolerance in government!

* Demand good education!

* Demand justice to those individuals violating our rights!!

* Demand good Police Protection

Please, *in the name of love:* ***unite all hearts for peace.***

Uleyma Weerakkody,

CEO founder of The Lighthouse, A non-profit to help battered women and men

As a daughter of a battered woman, I understood the importance of having a college education.

I believed if my mother had a higher level of education, she would have never endured that abuse.

We are living in times of hardship. Let's not forget to extend a hand to our neighbors, our friends. Reach out to friends we haven't spoken to in a while, a simple message "how are you" or "I'm here if you need to talk to someone."

I strongly believe in freedom of speech, peacefully and respecting others property.

"We have flown the air like birds and swum the sea like fishes but have yet learn the simple act of walking the earth like brothers." --Martin Luther King Jr

Steve Strachan,

Tax Professional,

Real Estate Investor

I currently own a tax business and am a real estate investor. I wanted to take a moment to speak to you about your future and finding your purpose. I was asked to share a little bit of my background.

I come from the world of advertising, where I produced Super Bowl commercials. When that industry shifted, I shifted into real estate and made a lot of money. That was great until it wasn't.

Then I shifted into big global business expansion. Currently, I have several businesses including a tax business.

The best advice that I can give to anybody, whether they're in school or in trade school, or trying to find themselves is first identify your passion and your purpose. That way, no matter what you do, you're receiving in your heart what you are called to do. Then in turn, as you bless others, that will prove to be invaluable for you. So many times, people get stuck in jobs because they think they must, or they become addicted to a paycheck.

My opinion on being an employee or having a job, you know, there's a distinction between a job and a career. If you have a job, it's something you do just to chase a paycheck. Don't ever do that.

There's one reason to be an employee in any given company and that's because you want to own a company like the one you work for. To truly get ahead in life, to win the game, you need to own a business and build something that you control. Never trust anybody else.

Go to school because your heart tells you this is what you're supposed to do. Don't go just to get a degree. Formal education is invaluable, but debt is detrimental. Be careful of falling into the trap that's been set for many students around the world. But most important, be connected to God and your Creator. By doing that, you'll find what your purpose is in your passion. Have a blessed day and have a blessed life.

Damon Jones,

U.S. Air Force Veteran, Creative Video Producer, TV/Video/Film Editor, FAA Licensed Aerial Drone Pilot/Instructor, Online Course Creator, and Author

I'm a proud husband and father who has truly found my purpose, passion, and peace through being a believer and follower of Jesus Christ. My life is focused on integrity and adding value to the lives of others.

I'm the owner of Purpose Video Services, a U.S. military veteran owned video production company that specializes in affordable and professional business related video production, FAA licensed aerial drone services, along with tv/film/ & video editing services. My services are based upon integrity, quality service, and follow up without compromise.

At the start of the pandemic in March 2020, I felt the need to share my personal testimony in a book—with full transparency—to help any boys and men who might be struggling with the issues associated with abandonment. The mission of my book, *Abandonment, The Plague of Most Men,* was written to share my life's testimony in the most transparent, open, and vulnerable way, to encourage other men from the age of eighteen to their golden years. Abandonment—an unfortunate plague affecting a lot of men is never really discussed transparently, but such a discussion is necessary for true healing. I went from being an angry boy to a prideful and stubborn male who masqueraded as a man. My anger was birthed by the bullying I endured from first grade through high school. My book is ultimately about me going from being bullied, to bullying, to becoming a servant soldier for Jesus Christ, because of a praying grandmother, mother, and wife. In the end, I finally learned to love Damon Jones, forgiven son of my Lord and Savior Jesus Christ. I had to embrace and accept the person I saw in the mirror every day. I accept myself for who I am and *whose* I am, despite what the world tells me.

I've learned from my life experiences that it's never too late to pursue your passion. I believe you're awesome and powerful! You can do whatever you put your mind to! We all have a God-given gift, but I had to humble myself and step out of my comfort zone and stop being paralyzed by my fears to recognize my gift. Everyone else around me recognized my gift, except me! But it's never too late! I share this with all transparency because I want you to live your life with even more fulfillment. You can do it! We weren't created just to exist, but to be of service to others. Don't let your fears paralyze you; allow them to propel you in the direction calling you from deep within.

Get out of fear and confidently believe in yourself despite whatever the people and the circumstances have dictated to you. Believe in yourself and you will be unstoppable.

Mai Segev,

World Traveler, Magik Maker, Free Thinker, married to the most amazing man and unschooling mom

I know this book is meant to encourage you to stay in school, however I'm suggesting the (not) radical idea that *you really don't need school at all!* (and hopefully you'll spare this outdated institute from you kids).

The brilliant Mark Twain sums it up beautifully: "I have never let schooling interfere with my education."

We've been indoctrinated from a young age to believe that education is important, and that the *only* place to get it is in schools.

As far as the first part of the sentence '*education*' is *not* important. *Knowledge*, however, is most important.

What's the difference? There are many people in the world who have lots of certificates hanging on the wall 'proving' they got plenty of education, yet they possess little knowledge. Equally, many people with no formal education at all are very knowledgeable.

Now let's address the second part: if you ask people why school exists, you're likely to hear that **School exists to give you knowledge.** And though it might have been true in the past (also debatable, but for another time), this argument is now irrelevant for two reasons:

1. You can learn anything - from history to math to art to programing to cooking to economics - online and by reading a vast array of essays and books. You don't need to go to 'school'.

2. The so called 'knowledge' taught in school has been proven as misleading (history is one example) and outdated as the world progresses much faster.

So really, **school exists to give you a certificate to hang on your wall.**

For schools to stay relevant they must teach you *how to learn*:

1. **Critical thinking** - so you can sort through the amount of information available and find facts (as opposed to opinions and misleading, twisted beliefs phrased as facts).

2. **Memory** - How to train your brain to absorb more information, retain it, and access it on demand.

3. **Focus** - How to stay focused in the age of distractions. (social media anyone?)

And give you *hands-on experience at life skills*:

1. **Permaculture** - How to grow food, using the natural eco-system we live in.

2. **Building** - How to build houses that support the environment and last longer.

3. **Sawing, Shoe making, Carpentering**, and so on…

It's been proven time and again that you learn better and faster when you *do* something (hands on experience) than when you only read or listen, so although understanding theory and history and the why behind it is important, by itself it amounts to nothing.

In other words, you can learn all the music theory in the world, yet you still won't be able to play an instrument.

You can pick up an instrument and practice playing without understanding any music theory at all.

You don't need school to practice - you just need to practice.

You don't need school to learn music theory - you can read books.

Same goes for practically any topic you wish to learn.

Following your curiosity gets you motivated to learn and read and practice. And when you're interested in a topic you retain more information and keep it longer.

AnGele Cade,

CEO, Entrepreneur, Public Speaker and Business Coach

From the moment I stepped on the UCLA campus 27 years ago, so many opportunities arose, relationships were created, and moments of transition occurred. I knew the road ahead wasn't going to be easy, but it was worth it. I remember the independence, the professors, the challenges, and especially the late nights.

It goes without saying, the challenges of today are much different from mine. Though there have been advances in technology and resources, navigating this season as a student is no easy feat. However, during these trying times it is important to stay true to your journey.

Your journey is a road that is taken by you to accomplish your goals and fulfill your passion. Don't give up on the accomplishment ahead. You deserve to finish what you have started, no matter if in person, in class, in hallways, in dorms, on couches, at desks, or on laptops while sitting on your bed. Many times, people embark on a journey only to be distracted by things that don't matter.

What is important to you? What will have a long-term impact on your goals? Without a doubt, you are a part of a generation of young adults equipped for the innovation, creativity, adjustments and inevitably the work ahead.

As I reflect on 2020, I can't help but think of the pandemic, the virus, the stay-at-home order, the social distancing, the politics, and the impact it's had on the entire world.

The year has been filled with devastation, loss, and the unexpected to say the very least. As I think about my family, my community, and the clients I service, inconvenient and heartbreaking are two words that come to mind. Worldwide, my clients, along with every other small business in our nation and beyond, have been placed on a curfew, forced to close their doors, discover new ways to connect to clients or even unable to work upon the onset of the virus.

Additionally, I believe the pandemic has revealed underlying social pandemics that have quietly plagued our nation for some time now - whether discovered through poverty, evictions, unemployment, or centuries of social tension produced by racism, judgements, or assumptions.

It's so easy to only consider the negative impact of this year, but in my opinion, it's necessary to also consider the space the pandemic has given us all. Some have found clarity to explore passions, space to pursue purpose, time for family and opportunity for rest. The pandemic has taken and, in a sense, given too, and my hope is that we take every gift - even in this moment we can change our perspective.

The problem is protesting, really, the issue is the combination of voices of people frustrated with the state of the status quo. Problems begin to protest online, in the streets, in government and to anyone who will listen. It is the rumbling of those that will no longer tolerate the knee of injustice on the neck of those that plead for a breath.

While I do not agree with riots unless it is targeted to the unjust, protests are necessary historically for real change in society, community, and country. Economic impact is the only thing that gets the attention. When traffic is halted, when streets are blocked and people are inconvenienced, then we have dialogue. In my opinion, protest is the preposition to conversation which is the prelude to action and the precipice of change.

Do you protest? Do you ignore it? Do you support it? Do you advocate? Do you make a change? Do you stand for the space of betterment? Let's make change together and focus on the solution.

AJ Heinicke,

AKA: AJSTUNTZ,

Actor, Model, Motorcycle Stunt Rider, Rapper, Humanitarian, Entrepreneur, Full-time Student 12 years old living with my parents in San Mateo. California

Let me tell you a little bit about myself.

I enjoy riding my Harley Davidson motorcycle, doing stunts on my Honda dirt bike, I enjoy wheeling and riding my bicycle. I have two music videos out and am working on my third song now. I am a huge kid humanitarian. I give back and support my community on a regular basis. Once a month I do a collaboration with "The City Eats" organization and we make sandwiches and lunches and give them out to the homeless and anyone in need throughout the San Francisco Bay Area. I also partner with my parents and we give back once a month, going directly to the streets and donating food and clothing to the homeless in San Mateo county and San Francisco. We bring dog sweaters and dog food and poop bags to the dogs out there with their owners on the street. We also raise money for various non-profits in need of help.

I made a strong partnership with the local children's homeless shelter in San Mateo "First Step-Life Moves" after I got to volunteer at the shelter with my mom and dad. I got to see how blessed I was and wanted to give back and support other kids. So, I created a calendar of myself and sell them for $10.00 each and all the proceeds go directly to the shelter. I have been doing this every year since the age of 8 years old and raise about $3,500 each year.

One of my biggest accomplishments is going on the Ellen Show and I not only got to meet Ellen but got to talk about donating my hair to kids with cancer through "Locks of Love" and even got to show Ellen my motorcycle stunt riding in her studio parking lot. Here is the link if you are interested in viewing it.

I am a kid entrepreneur. I am always talking to people and building and networking. Yes networking. I learned from a young age how to collaborate. I might be only 12 years old but I'm putting in the work. I am all about reaching for a new opportunity. Let's talk. I am AJSTUNTZ.

And as far as school, I am a typical kid. So sure, at first my thoughts are school? Well? It truly is one of those things in life we know will benefit us in the long run, so we do it. Plus, our parents remind us to do it. HAHAHA!!!

But when you really start to put it in focus and think deep about it: Ok school makes sense. I need to know how to read and understand contracts when I get that deal for my music. I need to know math skills, so I know you are paying me right. HAHAHAHA!!! I need Science and History and Social Studies, so I know how the world works around me. And being in school with other kids and teachers you socialize, not only meet them but learn from their experiences in life. What are they doing? How can I learn from this? The way I look at it. I had to think how this is going to benefit me -thinking positive, right. It makes going to school a bit easier when you look at it in a different way. Every day I go to school is a step closer to graduating.

My hopes are "People start to realize we are one community" and "We need to come together, look out for one another." Truly remember that it's great to give during the holidays but also remember everyone needs to eat every day. No-one should be sleeping outside in the cold.

David Roberti,

Founder and Director of EASE Arts in Action Grammys/MusiCares Facilitator CADCII

I am very inspired to hear Rosalyn's efforts and passion for her service and mission as well as the efforts and success of her students. Looking to tomorrow and the leaders for tomorrow resonates as a shining topic, which is, "Be Authentic," which gives leaders the ability to be mentally, physically, and spiritually fit.

Working with diverse populations, I have found a common thread that works universally to find balance through two things: love and acceptance. Having balance in one's life means you're living authentically, creating real value within and throughout your community, but above all doing the things that you love. This is how an individual becomes a tenant of a well-lived life.

Then we must look at acceptance, which is the key to seeing the truth as it is. This perspective resonates in your mind and all around you. Through action we show and convey our love and perspective to those who surround us.

Above all though, two things remain constant; change always happens, and we always have a choice to make. To acknowledging that change happens and to be part of a positive life, we must choose actions and make decisions that resonate self-esteem, sustainability in developing positivity, and enriching relationships. I've always been a advocate for a well-lived life, not only for myself but also my clients.

What Polonius says is true, *"To thine own self be true."* Be true to yourself and have a good time doing it.

Andrew Heller,

Life-long learner, yellow brick road follower, humorist, philosopher, poet, and visionary, Author/Screenwriter, Producer *A Gift of the Heart*

I was graciously asked to send a message from my purview to those who are up and coming in life. This is to guide you through the hurdles of life ahead.

I have noted, having read everyone else's view and advice, that they spent the first paragraph or so speaking about themselves and their accomplishments to qualify their opinion. I have chosen to leave that until the last and immediately launch a view that might, at times, feel disjointed and uncomfortable. However, if you make it to the end you will understand the point of view.

Life is a journey. Keeping that in mind, your journey, if you are just venturing out from school or are still in it, has only just begun. All the books, the professors, the academics will impress on you that learning is the be all and end all that need to live the rest of your life.

Wrong! Nothing can replace 'On the street' learning, the in the trenches, digging and fighting you will face day to day. Learning is just that, a guide to what you might expect and to give you an understanding of some of what might come at you.

Unfortunately, besides the fact that everything you learn is valuable, when a bat flies in your face you are ill equipped to quantify your response. I don't discount that what you learn is not valuable, it most certainly is. I encourage to seek it out at every opportunity.

That all being said, how do you find your way forward. It's simple when you take the time to sit down and cogitate (think deeply) about where you are and where exactly you would like to end up. You will find a myriad of opportunities at first along with a plethora of decisions which will seem daunting and untenable. But, through it all, you will find a path that feels right, comfortable, and definitive. This may or may not last for a while. As life changes, so shall your choices, your decisions, and your focus.

Here is the best advice, perhaps redundant, I can give you. If you are happy doing what you do, regardless of the monetary gain, the benefits that you accumulate as a result, then you have something money cannot buy. It is better to live a simple life filled with happiness than one that is miserably filled with anxiety trying to keep your financial status up with those who qualify you by that standard.

Pandemics aside! Life comes at you, bare knuckled without apology and without regret. Face life with a smile, with humility, with concern and kindness for those around you and that which you project shall return to you a millionfold. Learn to forgive and forget those who cannot keep up with you. Don't allow them the opportunity to hurt you, but if you harbor hate, regret, and retribution, that internal cancer will do more damage to you than them.

Live, love, be humble and as best you can be a leader, a light for good and not a dark cloud of vengeance. It is all a choice. You can change, but you cannot change someone else. Live for yourself and those close. Therein lies your future and any 'Pandemics,' physical, emotional, and financial that will at some point attack your life. It's not how you fight! Its ultimately how you smile and rise above it all with your God given grace which every single one of you have inside you if you just take a hot second to look.

Again, I will learn till the day I die. I love who I am, and I love life. Whatever it brings I shall climb its mountains, I will scream from the hilltops and I shall enjoy that which life will always teach me. Live well, live strong and believe in you and be the best part of you, you can be, if you just believe.

Now a short list of my qualifications: I'm 59, have travelled almost everywhere, learned cultures, history, and language. I have endured hardships you will hopefully never encounter in your life, or at least I hope you don't. Trust me when I say, life is a never-ending yellow brick road of knowledge and experience. Sometimes magical, sometimes scary. Sometimes we will be cowardly, sometimes we will have no heart, sometimes we will live with regret as our decisions were not right because 'We didn't have a brain.' Ultimately in the end, we will find the Emerald city and pass on to greatness as simply as a man behind a curtain and a dog, when all we want to do is go home. None of us can walk on water.

Find peace in everything you do right and everything you do wrong as everything is still a learning pathway to the future. Launch forward, unafraid and with utmost confidence, that right or wrong, you will survive and ultimately be better for it. Finally, share what you have learned to those that come behind you. Their journey has only just begun.

Until my eyes are dark and until my ears cannot hear I will always listen, see the future, and learn. Bless you all.

Marneen Lynne Fields,

Music Artist, Composer, Scriptwriter, Actress

I'm an award-winning pop-blues/soft-rock adult contemporary artist, ASCAP composer, scriptwriter, SAG/AFTRA actress, Hollywood stuntwoman, director, and author. I've appeared in 150 films, primetime TV shows, web series, music videos, and theatrical productions since 1976 working with some of the most famous actors, directors, and producers in the entertainment industry. I'm the CEO and creative director of Heavenly Waterfall Song Publishing and Productions Company. I'm severely hearing impaired.

In 1973 I was one of three women in the United States to receive an athletic scholarship in gymnastics to Utah State University where I was the #1 class one advanced all-around gymnast for the college, ranked 3rd in the nation in intercollegiate competition. Olympic gold medalist Olga Korbut's book *Olga* changed my life at nineteen years old when she taught me, "The competition is within, not with others." After a tragic fall off the balance beam in 1976, I underwent an ankle reconstruction surgery where a calf's tendon was inserted into my foot in place of my human ligaments. I was discovered by Hollywood later that year fresh off my ankle surgery, and by 1977 I was one of the most famous young stunt women in the world. By 1985 I was coined Hollywood's Original Fall Girl and awarded a "Fall Girl" license plate.

I'm honored that I've been asked by Rosalyn Kahn and Maryel McKinney to contribute a feature in this book. I stand before you today to inspire you with a champion athlete's mindset that your dreams are obtainable no matter what obstacles you might face throughout your life. All you need is a focused creative imagination where you can free yourself to visualize and brainstorm with yourself all possibilities. Think outside the box to learn what reaching your highest potential might mean to you. These are your goals and dreams, and they are no one else's business but yours and God's. What do you think God created you to do? What lifts your soul? What brings joy?

I'm the author of the 5-Star rated book, *The Illusive Craft of Acting: An Actor's Preparation Process*. As an actor when you're creating a character you ask yourself questions like, "Who am I?" "What do I want?" "How am I going to go about getting it?" Spend time with yourself creating a strong foundation of faith in your talents with an unwavering belief in the attainment of your goals. There is nothing you can't achieve that you set your mind to if you work hard to achieve it.

Next year I'm looking forward to publishing two books about my life and career, *Cartwheels & Halos: The True Marneen Lynne Fields Story*, and *Rollin' with the Punches: An Examination of the Stunt and Acting Careers of Marneen Fields.* In 1988, I barely survived a horrific car accident where I fought for my life for a decade and underwent a series of life-threatening abdominal operations. I lost everything that I had worked for and was famous for and that I loved. I lost all my gymnastic and stunt talent. I had to face the reality that I would never be able to have a child, and I cried and cried. Miraculously, I found something much more valuable during this tragedy. I found God, and one day during prayer I found my true calling in the wake of my childhood dream of music.

It might be darkest before the dawn world-wide right now trying to cope during a pandemic, but it doesn't have to put out the light in your heart to get creative with what you see yourself doing for the rest of your life. Become a leader not a follower. March to your own drum beat of how you would like to make a difference in this world. God bless you.

Michael Coulombe,

Writer/Director, Photographer, Former Student

My name is Michael Coulombe. Presently I work in the film industry. I am a writer/director as well as a photographer.

I know in these difficult and trying times it can be hard to be motivated. Trust me, I fight it every day. With so much false information thrown about it is hard to believe or know what is factual. I do know this. The virus is real as I have known people who have suffered from it and died from it and I know that it has disrupted life as we know it, or rather, as we *KNEW* it. What this pandemic and subsequent lockdown has shown us is that we need to take a step back and perhaps re-evaluate the way in which we have conducted ourselves and our place within the world.

That sounds a bit existential, I know. What I mean is that, with these new restrictions put on our daily lives, we need to find new ways in which to survive…in which to live….in which to go about our regular routine. And amazing how quickly we adapt, right? Where we used to have in class learning, we now educate online. Same with board meetings, dance recitals, doctor visits, even graduations and family reunions.

We used to talk about the future – the future is now!

I think, though, to understand the future, we need to learn from the past. When the protests and riots first happened at the beginning of the pandemic, my mother said something to me. She said it in passing but it stuck with me for several days, "All of these protests remind of what we saw in the 60s."

Keep in mind we are now in 2020 – which means that this is almost 60 years later. Reminds me of the phrase "If you don't learn from history, then you are doomed to repeat it." Have we not learned anything?

Or perhaps we have learned something and are finally at a point where we can do something about it. Watching the video of George Floyd being brutally attacked by the cops shows us where we stand as a country when it comes to race. The man did nothing. He was handcuffed and sat on the ground and a man, a cop, sat on his neck LONG after he was dead, just because he could, because he was taught that it was okay to do so. Yet, a 17- year-old white kid can cross state lines carrying an illegal firearm, kill two people, and get treated like a hero.

I am a white man, and this breaks my heart. It hurts me that people can hate so much that they can justify murder. I grew up gay. I know what it is like to be on the receiving end of that hate. It is scary, really scary. It is a fear and revulsion that is so engrained in their psyche, so entrenched in their DNA, that they are able to walk away and feel vindicated, as if they rid the world of a plague.

So, to me, these protests are warranted, these protests are needed. I have marched in protests in the past and I marched in protests in 2020. People were there for me when I needed a voice. I am there for them when they need a voice. I can be their voice!

I think the true question is: When we look back 10 years from now, 20 years from now, 30 years from now, what side of history do you want to be on?

Dr. Maryel McKinley Ph.D., Public Figure

Addictions Counselor, Mentor, Advocate, #1 Arbitron-rated Talk Radio Show Host/Producer in Los Angeles on 97.1 FM KSLX, Winner of West Publishing's Contract Law Award, Dog Lover

Maryel McKinley with Princess, her Service Schnauzer
dr.maryelmckinley.com

When Rosalyn Kahn, my friend and prodigy, and host of a TV show I help produce, asked me to write my message to you, Tomorrow's Leaders, for this book I decided to share with you that I have lived with a serious disabling disease my entire adult life and have overcome addiction, co-dependency, and PTSD, living one day at a time, for years.

For a long time, I couldn't leave the house without Princess, my PTSD service dog (shown with me above). Through it all, I never let obstacles discourage me. Rather, they inspire me!

Before the world went into lockdown, I was already doing telephone appointments with my doctor and the experts at my HMO.

Why?

I've had a rare chronic strain of Hep C genome #3A for over four decades, like fighting off the flu virus every day of your life for 40 years! Unfortunately, one of the secondary issues is a lowered immune system.

Living with this disease, which was supposed to have killed me 20 years ago, is severely disabling. Sometimes if I catch an infection or flu it can leave me near death. For instance, I went on hospice after a surgery in 2017 to cut out an infection in my right hip.

Since I was five years old, when I appeared on my first Network TV show, my driving factor has been to utilize the power of all forms of media to spread healing and a message of love, hope and inspiration.

When I was 12, I embraced a powerful quote from Norman Vincent Peale's *Power of Positive Thinking* that became the mantra I live by: "For every adversity there is a seed of equal or greater opportunity."

This quote helped me overcome immense personal challenges, disabilities, and extreme adversity throughout my many years on the planet.

I'm amazed when I look back and see how much I've accomplished:

Second chair violinist touring at age 15 with the SFV Symphony Orchestra Bicentennial Tour Album.

Touring in Ice Capades Show Continental Co. as a professional ice skater.

Being a Casting Director at Computer-Casting, the first Computerized Casting Agency.

The Lead and Co-star in two Movies and appearing in commercials as IMDB/SAG stage name Mary McKinley.

Writing Songs & Lyrics for Hudson Bay Publishing in NYC.

Being published in print magazines.

Being a Print Model on two back covers of Show Biz Magazine in New York and a Runway Model for designer Chinese Laundry in Los Angeles and New York City.

Being a single mother.

Going back to school to study Chemical Dependency Counseling, then to Graduate school for Law and finally a PhD.

Faculty member and Addictions expert for Deepak Chopra's *My Potential.*

Being asked to appear on Oprah, Tyra Banks, and Ricki Lake as an Addictions expert.

Having a #1 Rated Arbitron rated "All Talk Recovery Radio" CBS 97.1 FM KLSX Los Angeles as well as KABC's Back-Talk Los Angeles

Through all these accomplishments, I struggled with serious disabilities and overcame them.

My message to you: Never let adversity get in the way of accomplishing your dreams. I pray my journey will inspire you to find your greatness!

Have a sense of humor as laughter's the best RX medicine when all else fails! Life has a funny sense of humor so don't take yourself too seriously and dream big!

Albert Einstein said, "You can't solve the problem at the level of the problem."

Learn to "Get out of the Problem and into the solution." Live with an open mind, a compassionate heart, personal integrity, and a giving spirit, ask what you can add to the stream of life rather than follow those always on the take. See my article at https://renascent.ca/getting-problem-solution/

Then add a Higher Power like a Loving God into that equation.

You will succeed no matter what stands in your way!

Finally, surround yourself with winners, get a mentor and be a mentor. Volunteer as much as you can and if you need help with an addiction-related issue -contact me and I will freely give what was freely given to me.

May God bless your journey!

www.ingramcontent.com/pod-product-compliance
Lightning Source LLC
LaVergne TN
LVHW010933110826
845149LV00013B/2576

9780999649794